CW00427966

by Iain Gray

LangSyne
PUBLISHING
WRITING *to* REMEMBER

Lang**Syne**

PUBLISHING

WRITING *to* REMEMBER

79 Main Street, Newtongrange,
Midlothian EH22 4NA
Tel: 0131 344 0414   Fax: 0845 075 6085
E-mail: info@lang-syne.co.uk
www.langsyneshop.co.uk

Design by Dorothy Meikle
Printed by Ricoh Print Scotland
© Lang Syne Publishers Ltd 2014

ISBN 978-1-85217-640-2

Bailey

MOTTO:

One's country is where one is well.

CREST:

A black boar's head.

NAME variations include:

Bailie

Bailley

Baillie

Bayllie

Bayley

Baly

Chapter one:

The origins of popular surnames

by George Forbes and Iain Gray

If you don't know where you came from, you won't know where you're going **is a frequently quoted observation and one that has a particular resonance today when there has been a marked upsurge in interest in genealogy, with increasing numbers of people curious to trace their family roots.**

Main sources for genealogical research include census returns and official records of births, marriages and deaths – and the key to unlocking the detail they contain is obviously a family surname, one that has been 'inherited' and passed from generation to generation.

No matter our station in life, we all have a surname – but it was not until about the middle of the fourteenth century that the practice of being identified by a particular surname became commonly established throughout the British Isles.

Previous to this, it was normal for a person to be identified through the use of only a forename.

But as population gradually increased and there were many more people with the same forename, surnames were adopted to distinguish one person, or community, from another.

Many common English surnames are patronymic in origin, meaning they stem from the forename of one's father – with 'Johnson,' for example, indicating 'son of John.'

It was the Normans, in the wake of their eleventh century conquest of Anglo-Saxon England, a pivotal moment in the nation's history, who first brought surnames into usage – although it was a gradual process.

For the Normans, these were names initially based on the title of their estates, local villages and chateaux in France to distinguish and identify these landholdings.

Such grand descriptions also helped enhance the prestige of these warlords and generally glorify their lofty positions high above the humble serfs slaving away below in the pecking order who had only single names, often with Biblical connotations as in Pierre and Jacques.

The only descriptive distinctions among the peasantry concerned their occupations, like 'Pierre the swineherd' or 'Jacques the ferryman.'

Roots of surnames that came into usage in England not only included Norman-French, but also Old French, Old Norse, Old English, Middle English, German, Latin, Greek, Hebrew and the Gaelic languages of the Celts.

The Normans themselves were originally Vikings, or 'Northmen', who raided, colonised and eventually settled down around the French coastline.

The had sailed up the Seine in their longboats in 900AD under their ferocious leader Rollo and ruled the roost in north eastern France before sailing over to conquer England in 1066 under Duke William of Normandy – better known to posterity as William the Conqueror, or King William I of England.

Granted lands in the newly-conquered England, some of their descendants later acquired territories in Wales, Scotland and Ireland – taking not only their own surnames, but also the practice of adopting a surname, with them.

But it was in England where Norman rule and custom first impacted, particularly in relation to the adoption of surnames.

This is reflected in the famous *Domesday Book*, a massive survey of much of England and Wales, ordered by William I, to determine who owned what, what it was worth and therefore how much they were liable to pay in taxes to the voracious Royal Exchequer.

Completed in 1086 and now held in the National Archives in Kew, London, 'Domesday' was an Old English word meaning 'Day of Judgement.'

This was because, in the words of one contemporary chronicler, "its decisions, like those of the Last Judgement, are unalterable."

It had been a requirement of all those English landholders – from the richest to the poorest – that they identify themselves for the purposes of the survey and for future reference by means of a surname.

This is why the *Domesday Book*, although written in Latin as was the practice for several centuries with both civic and ecclesiastical records, is an invaluable source for the early appearance of a wide range of English surnames.

Several of these names were coined in connection with occupations.

These include Baker and Smith, while Cooks, Chamberlains, Constables and Porters were to be found carrying out duties in large medieval households.

The church's influence can be found in names such as Bishop, Friar and Monk while the popular name of Bennett derives from the late fifth to mid-sixth century Saint Benedict, founder of the Benedictine order of monks.

The early medical profession is represented by Barber, while businessmen produced names that include Merchant and Sellers.

Down at the village watermill, the names that cropped up included Millar/Miller, Walker and Fuller, while other self-explanatory trades included Cooper, Tailor, Mason and Wright.

Even the scenery was utilised as in Moor, Hill, Wood and Forrest – while the hunt and the chase supplied names that include Hunter, Falconer, Fowler and Fox.

Colours are also a source of popular surnames, as in Black, Brown, Gray/Grey, Green and White, and would have denoted the colour of the clothing the person habitually wore or, apart from the obvious exception of 'Green', one's hair colouring or even complexion.

The surname Red developed into Reid, while

Blue was rare and no-one wanted to be associated with yellow.

Rather self-important individuals took surnames that include Goodman and Wiseman, while physical attributes crept into surnames such as Small and Little.

Many families proudly boast the heraldic device known as a Coat of Arms, as featured on our front cover.

The central motif of the Coat of Arms would originally have been what was borne on the shield of a warrior to distinguish himself from others on the battlefield.

Not featured on the Coat of Arms, but highlighted on page three, is the family motto and related crest – with the latter frequently different from the central motif.

Adding further variety to the rich cultural heritage that is represented by surnames is the appearance in recent times in lists of the 100 most common names found in England of ones that include Khan, Patel and Singh – names that have proud roots in the vast sub-continent of India.

Echoes of a far distant past can still be found in our surnames and they can be borne with pride in commemoration of our forebears.

Chapter two:

Conquest and civil war

To trace the origins of the Bailey name in England, we have to travel back through the dim mists of time to Normandy – because this is from where it mainly derives, along with other popular spelling variants that include 'Bailley' and 'Baillie.'

Originally an occupational surname, it denoted someone entrusted with high civic office, such as a steward or sheriff, and derives from the Late Latin 'baiulives' and the Norman 'bailiff', meaning 'to deliver.'

In addition to being an occupational name, 'Bailey' and its spelling variants may also have a locational association with Bailleul-en-Vimeu in the Somme region of Normandy.

Yet other possible sources of derivation are from the Old French 'baile', or 'baille', denoting 'enclosure' – such as the outer courtyard of a castle and known in Middle English as a 'baile', or 'bailly' – and it is from this that the London courts of justice known as the Old Bailey, whose site once formed part of an outer wall of the city derives.

Some authorities also highlight the Old English 'berry' and 'leah', combining to form 'bailey' and indicating a woodland clearing.

But it was undoubtedly in the wake of the Norman Conquest of England in 1066 that 'Bailey' and its variants became popularised as a surname.

By 1066, England had become a nation with several powerful competitors to the throne.

In what were extremely complex family, political and military machinations, the monarch was Harold II, who had succeeded to the throne following the death of Edward the Confessor.

But his right to the throne was contested by two powerful competitors – his brother-in-law King Harold Hardrada of Norway, in alliance with Tostig, Harold II's brother, and Duke William II of Normandy.

In what has become known as The Year of Three Battles, Hardrada invaded England and gained victory over the English king on September 20 at the battle of Fulford, in Yorkshire.

Five days later, however, Harold II decisively defeated his brother-in-law and brother at the battle of Stamford Bridge.

But he had little time to celebrate his victory,

having to immediately march south from Yorkshire to encounter a mighty invasion force, led by Duke William, that had landed at Hastings, in East Sussex.

Harold's battle-hardened but exhausted force of Anglo-Saxon soldiers confronted the Normans on October 14 in a battle subsequently depicted on the Bayeux tapestry – a 23ft. long strip of embroidered linen thought to have been commissioned eleven years after the event by the Norman Odo of Bayeux.

Harold drew up a strong defensive position at the top of Senlac Hill, building a shield wall to repel Duke William's cavalry and infantry.

The Normans suffered heavy losses, but through a combination of the deadly skill of their archers and the ferocious determination of their cavalry they eventually won the day.

Anglo-Saxon morale had collapsed on the battlefield as word spread through the ranks that Harold had been killed – the Bayeux Tapestry depicting this as having happened when the English king was struck by an arrow to the head.

Amidst the carnage of the battlefield, it was difficult to identify him – the last of the Anglo-Saxon kings.

Some sources assert William ordered his

body to be thrown into the sea, while others state it was secretly buried at Waltham Abbey.

What is known with certainty, however, is that William in celebration of his great victory founded Battle Abbey, near the site of the battle, ordering that the altar be sited on the spot where Harold was believed to have fallen.

William was declared King of England on December 25, and the complete subjugation of his Anglo-Saxon subjects followed.

Those Normans who had fought on his behalf were rewarded with the lands of Anglo-Saxons, many of whom sought exile abroad as mercenaries.

Within an astonishingly short space of time, Norman manners, customs and law were imposed on England – laying the basis for what subsequently became established 'English' custom and practice.

Among those Normans rewarded for their service to William was a bearer of the 'Bailey' name who was granted lands in Northumberland, in the far north of England – and subsequent bearers of the name came to stamp a mark on the frequently turbulent historical record.

In the tumultuous seventeenth century, Thomas Bailey, sometimes rendered as 'Bayly', was the Church of England clergyman who became embroiled in the bitter and bloody English Civil War.

King Charles I had incurred the wrath of Parliament by his insistence on the 'divine right' of monarchs, and added to this was Parliament's fear of Catholic 'subversion' against the state and the king's stubborn refusal to grant demands for religious and constitutional concessions.

Matters came to a head with the outbreak of the war in 1642, with Parliamentary forces, known as the New Model Army and commanded by Oliver Cromwell and Sir Thomas Fairfax, arrayed against the Royalist army of the king.

In what became an increasingly bloody and complex conflict, spreading to Scotland and Ireland and with rapidly shifting loyalties on both sides, Charles was eventually captured and executed in January of 1649 on the orders of Parliament.

Thomas Bailey, whose place and date of birth is not known, was a son of Lewis Bailey, or Bayly, Bishop of Bangor.

Educated at Magdalene College, Cambridge and, as a clergyman, appointed rector of Holgate, Shropshire in 1638, he took up arms for the Royalist cause and served as an officer in defence of the New

Model Army's siege in the summer of 1646 of the imposing fortress of Raglan Castle, near the village of Raglan in Monmouthshire, Wales.

The castle was held by Henry Somerset, 1st Marquess of Worcester, who had inherited it in 1628, and Bailey served as his chaplain.

The castle endured a lengthy siege until, in August of 1646, its defenders had to surrender after a Parliamentary force commanded by Sir Thomas Fairfax battered it into submission – not least through the deployment of a mighty cannon known as "Roaring Meg."

Thomas Bailey appears to have escaped imprisonment at this time, but the Marquess was imprisoned in Windsor Castle, where he died only a short time afterwards.

Three years later, and still a staunch defender of the ill-fated Charles, Bailey was imprisoned for a time in London's Newgate Prison after penning a stinging attack on Parliament following the monarch's execution; he died in 1657.

Chapter three:

Fame and infamy

Far removed from the turbulence of civil war, bearers of the Bailey name have achieved distinction through a colourful range of rather more peaceful endeavours and pursuits.

Not only a South African diamond tycoon but also a financier, art collector, cricketer and philanthropist, Sir Abraham "Abe" Bailey was born in 1864 in Cradock, Eastern Cape.

Of English descent through his father and Scottish descent through his mother, he was educated in England.

Showing a flair for business, he quickly acquired diamond mining and land properties in the former Rhodesia, now Zimbabwe, and so extensive did his holdings become that by the 1930s he was recognised as one of the world's wealthiest men.

Maintaining homes in both Cape Town and in London and having been raised to the Peerage in 1910, he was one of a number of immensely wealthy "Randlords" – named from the South African currency – honoured for their service to the British Empire.

As a talented cricketer, he played for Transvaal, while as an art collector – particularly of sporting art – the bulk of his impressive collection was displayed in his London home.

Following his death in 1940, under his will the Sir Abe Bailey Bequest was established and his collection of prints, paintings and drawings transferred into the care of the National Gallery in Cape Town.

Twenty-six years his junior, his second wife was the intrepid and pioneering aviatrix – as female aviators are known – Dame Mary Bailey.

Born at Rossmore Castle in Co. Monaghan, daughter of the Anglo-Irish Derrick Warner William Westenra, 5th Baron Rossmore, she was aged 21 when she married Bailey.

Taking to the skies and awarded a pilot's licence in 1927, in 1928 she made a solo flight from Croydon, London, to Cape Town in a de Havilland Cirrus Mothwith, and then back again while in the same year she set a world height record, piloting a light aircraft to a height of 17,283ft .

Twice winner, in 1927 and 1928, of the Harmon Trophy as "the world's outstanding aviatrix", she served with the Women's Royal Auxiliary Air Force during the Second World War.

Appointed Dame Commander of the Order of the British Empire (DBE), she died in 1960.

She was the mother of Sir Derrick Bailey, 3rd Baronet, who inherited his parents' passion for both aviation and cricket.

Born in 1918 in London, he was awarded the Distinguished Flying Cross (DFC) during the Second World War for gallantry and devotion to duty while serving as a pilot with the South African Air Force in No. 223 Squadron (RAF), while as a cricketer he played for Gloucestershire.

Later settling in Guernsey, in the Channel Islands, and setting up Aurigny Air Services to operate between Guernsey and Alderney, he died in 2009.

In the world of science and invention, Jacob Whitman Bailey was the American naturalist and pioneer of microscopic research born in 1811 in Auburn, Massachusetts.

In his lifetime a professor in three separate disciplines – chemistry, geology and mineralogy – he invented a number of improvements to the microscope that allowed for even closer scrutiny and greater clarity of microscopic samples.

Appointed president of the American

Association for the Advancement of Science shortly before his death in 1857, he was also an Associate Fellow of the American Arts and Sciences.

A toolmaker and an inventor, Leonard Bailey lends his name to the Stanley/Bailey planes used in woodworking to this day.

Born in 1825 in Hollis, New Hampshire, many of his woodworking patents were taken up by the Stanley Rule and Level Company, now known as Stanley Works and based in New Britain, Connecticut; he died in 1905.

Recognised as one the most influential biochemical engineers of modern times, James Edward Bailey, better known as Jay Bailey, was born in 1944.

Noted for his work in the field of metabolic engineering in particular, the American scientist studied chemical engineering at Rice University, in Houston, Texas, before working for Shell and then holding other posts that included teaching chemical engineering at the University of Houston.

Appointed professor of biotechnology at the Swiss Federal Institute of Technology in 1992, he died in 2001 while he is commemorated through the annual James E. Bailey Award for

Outstanding Contributions to the Field of Biological Engineering.

Noted for having played a vital role in securing Allied victory during the Second World War, Sir Donald Coleman Bailey was the English civil engineer who invented the Bailey Bridge.

Born in Rotherham, Yorkshire, in 1901 and having studied at The Leys School, Cambridge and Sheffield University, he was a civil servant in the War Office when he designed the bridge that bears his name.

A portable, prefabricated, truss structure requiring no special heavy equipment or tools to construct and strong enough to carry tanks, it proved indispensable to Allied military engineering units.

Knighted in 1946 for his contribution to the war effort, he died in 1985, while after the war British Field Marshall Bernard Montgomery stated: "Without the Bailey Bridge, we should not have won the war."

One particularly infamous bearer of the otherwise proud name of Bailey was Harvey Bailey, known as "The Dean of American Robbers."

Born in 1887 in West Virginia, from 1920 to 1933 he robbed a number of banks across America and is thought to have netted an estimated total of more than $1m.

Caught and imprisoned in Kansas State Prison in 1932, he escaped in a mass breakout in June of the following year.

But he was recaptured by chance only a few weeks later by FBI officers investigating a kidnapping that made media headlines.

Known as the Urschel Kidnapping, it involved the kidnapping on July 22, 1933, of the wealthy Texan oilman Charles Frederick Urschel by the notorious gangster George "Machine Gun Kelly" Barnes and his partner in crime Albert L. Bates.

The pair kidnapped Urschel at the point of a machine-gun, in front of his terrified wife, from his residence in Oklahoma City and took him to a farmhouse in Paradise, Texas.

He was held there for over a week until family representatives paid a $200,000 ransom in bills that the FBI had carefully ensured were documented.

Although Urschel had been blindfolded during most of his captivity, after his release he was nevertheless able to provide the FBI with important details that eventually led them to the farmhouse.

It was here that they arrested its owners,

Robert Shannon and his wife Ora and Harvey Bailey. The fugitive was using it as a safe house and had some of the dollar bills in his possession.

"Machine Gun Kelly", his wife Kathryn and Albert L. Bates were quickly tracked down and, along with Bailey and the Shannons, sentenced to life imprisonment.

After incarceration in various penal institutions that included Alcatraz, Bailey was finally released in 1964.

Only a few months short of his 92nd birthday, he died peacefully in Joplin, Missouri in 1979.

Chapter four:

On the world stage

In the creative art that is photography, David Bailey is the leading English fashion and portrait photographer born in 1938 in Leytonstone, East London.

The son of a tailor's cutter and a machinist, he has gained international acclaim after having surmounted the disadvantage of being born with dyslexia and the motor skill disorder known as developmental coordination disorder.

Leaving school when aged 15, his first job was as a copy boy in the Fleet Street offices of the *Yorkshire Post* newspaper, while in 1957 he served with the Royal Air Force during National Service.

His passion for photography came to the fore after he was demobbed, and he subsequently crafted his art while working for a time in London with the photographers David Ollins and John French.

Branching out on his own, he became a fashion photographer for *Vogue* magazine while, as a freelance, he became famous for his iconic images of the "Swinging London" of the 1960s.

His work during this period is showcased in his famous *Box of Pin-Ups* – a box of poster-prints featuring a colourful range of celebrities who include the Beatles, the model Jean Shrimpton, Mick Jagger, Andy Warhol and even the notorious London East End gangster twins Ronnie and Reggie Kray.

The recipient of a CBE in 2001 for services to art and, in 2005, the Royal Photographic Society's Centenary Medal and Honorary Fellowship, he was married for a time to the French actress Catherine Deneuve and the American fashion model Marie Helvin.

Bearers of the Bailey name have also excelled in the highly competitive world of sport.

On the squash court, **Tania Bailey** is the English professional player born in 1979 in Stamford, Lincolnshire.

Winner of the World Junior Championship in 1997, she overcame a serious knee injury sustained in a car accident when she was aged 21 to go on to win a silver medal in the women's doubles event at the 2002 Commonwealth Games, a bronze in the event at the 2006 games and, in the same year, winning the British National Championships.

On the athletics track, **Angela Bailey**, born in

1962, is the Canadian former track and field athlete who, with a time of 10.98 seconds, at the time of writing still holds the Canadian record for the 100-metres event.

This was achieved at the World Championships in 1987, while nine years earlier she won a silver medal as a member of the Canadian 4x100-metres relay team at the Commonwealth Games.

Also in Canadian athletics, **Donovan Bailey**, born in 1967 in Jamaica but immigrating to Canada when he was aged 13, is the retired sprinter who won a gold medal at the 1996 Olympics for both the 100-metres event and also in the 4x400-metres relay.

Still on the athletics track, **Aleen May Bailey** is the Jamaican track and field sprinter born in 1980 in St Mary.

Winner of a gold medal as a member of the Jamaican 4x100-metres relay team at the 2004 Olympics, she is a sister of the reggae and dancehall artist Clifton George Bailey III, better known as **Capleton**.

Born in St Mary in 1967 and also known as "King Shango", "King David", "The Fireman" and "The Prophet", he is known for a number of hits that include his 1992 *Alms House*.

In a much different musical genre, **Pearl Bailey** was the African-American singer and actress who in 1967, along with Cab Calloway, gained acclaim for their performances on Broadway in an all-black production of *Hello, Dolly!*

Born Pearl Mae Bailey in 1918 in Southampton County, Virginia, she won a Tony Award for the title role in *Hello, Dolly!* while in 1946 she had made her Broadway debut in a production of *St Louis Woman*.

Film credits include the 1954 *Carmen Jones* and the 1959 *Porgy and Bess*, while she hosted her own American television show during the 1970s.

The provider of voice animations for the 1976 *Tubby the Tuba* and Disney's 1981 *The Fox and the Hound*, she was also the author of a number of books that include *The Raw Pearl* and, from 1989, *Between You and Me*.

Appointed special ambassador to the United Nations by President Gerald Ford in 1975 and the recipient in 1988 of the Presidential Medal of Freedom from President Ronald Reagan, she died in 1990.

She was a sister of the famed tap-dancer **Bill Bailey**, the first person to be filmed performing what he called the Backslide – a dance movement later made more famous by Michael Jackson as the *Moonwalk*.

Born in 1912 and with film credits that include the 1943 *Cabin in the Sky*, starring beside Lena Horne and Ethel Waters, and having been trained by the equally famed tap-dancer Bill "Bojangles" Robinson, he died in 1978.

Known as "The Queen of Swing", "Mrs Swing" and "The Rockin' Chair Lady", Mildred Rinker Bailey was the top American jazz singer of the 1930s better known as **Mildred Bailey** – with 'Bailey' her married name.

Born in 1907 in Tekoa, Washington and later moving to Seattle, she went on to enjoy success with hits that include *Trust in Me*, *I Let a Song Go Out Of My Heart*, *Please Be Kind* and *Rockin' Chair*.

The sister of the lyricist Charles Rinker and the composer Al Rinker, she died in 1951.

Born in Philadelphia in 1933, Donald Orlando Bailey was the American jazz drummer better known as **Duck Bailey**.

Having played with other jazz greats including John Coltrane and known as "The King of Organ Trio Drummers", he died in 2013, while was an uncle of the bass guitarist **Victor Bailey**.

Born in Philadelphia in 1960 and now a successful solo artist, from 1982 to 1986 he played with the band Weather Report.

Born in 1979 in Leeds, West Yorkshire, **Corinne Bailey Rae**, born Corinne Jacqueline Bailey, is the British singer, songwriter and guitarist whose debut album *Corinne Bailey Rae* reached Number 1 in the UK charts in 2006.

Winner of a Grammy Award for Album of the Year for her work as a featured artist on Herbie Hancock's *River: The Joni Letters* and nominated for the 2010 Mercury Music Prize for Album of the Year for *The Sea* and in 2012, the recipient of a Grammy Award for *Is This Love*, she was married from 2001 until his death in 2008 to fellow musician Jason Rae.

Born in 1954 in Halifax, West Yorkshire, **Tom Bailey** is the musician best known for having been a founding member of the British new wave band Thompson Twins.

Along with fellow band members Alannah Currie and Joe Leeway, he had international success throughout the 1980s with hits that include *Hold Me Now* and *Lay Your Hands on Me*.

He now has achieved further success, along

with Alannah Currie, in the duo Babble, while he also performs under the name International Observer.

An inductee of America's Country Music Hall of Fame, **DeFord Bailey** was the country and blues star born in 1899 in Smith County, Tennessee.

Renowned for his harmonica tunes, he was the first African-American – in 1926 – to be featured as a performer on Nashville's *Grand Ole Opry* radio show.

Described by *The Encyclopaedia of Country Music* as "the most significant black country music star before World War II" and known for hits that include his 1927 *Pan American Blues*, he died in 1982.

Back on British shores and in contemporary times, Samantha Florence Bailey, better known as **Sam Bailey**, is the singer who in 2013 won the tenth series of the television music talent show *The X Factor*.

Born in 1977 in Bexley, London, and a former prison officer, her single *Skyscraper* became the Christmas 2103 top-selling UK single, while her album *The Power of Love* reached the No 1 spot a few months later.

Also on British shores, Mark Bailey, better known as **Bill Bailey**, is the musician, comedian, actor and author born in 1964 in Bath, Somerset.

A classically trained musician and ranked 7th in 2010 in Channel 4 television's list of "100 Greatest Stand-Ups", he is known for roles in television comedy series that include *Black Books* and also for appearances as a panellist on shows that include *QI*, *Never Mind the Buzzcocks* and *Have I Got News for You*.

Winner of the Best Live Stand-Up Award at the British Comedy Awards in 1999, he also has the rather unusual accolade of honorary membership of the Society of Crematorium Organists.

Also in the world of entertainment, George William Bailey, also known as **G.W. Bailey**, is the American actor known for his comedic roles in films and television series that include that of Captain Thaddeus Harris in *Police Academy* and of Staff Sergeant Luther Rizzo in *M*A*S*H*.

Born in 1944 in Port Arthur, Texas, he has also had a dramatic role from 2012 in the American television series *Major Crimes*.

Known for his roles in the television series *Dawson's Creek* and the Second World War drama

Band of Brothers, **Eion Bailey** is the American actor born in 1976 in Santa Ynez Valley, California.

On Australian shores, **Imogen Bailey** is the actress, model and singer, born in Canberra in 1977, known for her former role of Nicola West in the popular soap *Neighbours*.

Behind the camera lens, **Rob Bailey** is the English-born television director noted for his work on American television series that include *CSI: NY*, *CSI: Crime Scene Investigation* and *The Wire*.

Born in Sussex in 1966, **Ewan Bailey** is the English actor, voice actor and director whose radio credits include the BBC Radio 4 satire *The Sunday Format* and whose television credits include *Funland*, *Honest* and the series *Rome*.

As a noted documentary voice artist, he has also provided narration for a number of television channels that include Discovery.

In the equally creative world of the written word, **Paul Bailey** is the British critic, novelist and biographer known for works that include his 1982 biography *An English Madam: The Life and Work of Cynthia Payne* in addition to novels that include his 1967 *The Jerusalem*, winner of both an Arts Council Award and a Somerset Maughan Award.

Born in London in 1937, he is also the author of other acclaimed works that include his 1986 novel *Gabriel's Lament*, its 1993 sequel *Sugar Cane* and his 2000 biography *The Stately Homo: A Celebration of the Life of Quentin Crisp*.